CHIV
BOOK
CHILDREN'S
PARTIES

JANET WARREN

**MARTIN
BOOKS**

Contents

THE AUTHOR

Janet Warren's experience, both as a cookery writer and as a working mother, made her the ideal author for this book. She has numerous other cookery books to her name, including *The Microwave Way* (Sphere). Janet now works from home as a writer and cookery consultant, combining this with looking after her young sons.

NOTES

Ingredients are given in both metric and imperial measures. Use either set of quantities, but not a mixture of both, in any one recipe.
All spoon measurements are made using level British standard spoons.
Eggs are standard (size 3) unless otherwise stated.

Published by Martin Books
Simon & Schuster International Group
Fitzwilliam House 32 Trumpington Street
Cambridge CB2 1QY

First published 1989
© Woodhead-Faulkner (Publishers) Ltd 1989

ISBN 0 85941 444 2

Party planning

A party wouldn't be a party without jelly, and Chivers jellies have been making a hit at the best children's parties for years. Now they have asked me to put together a book that will tell you all you need to know to make the next party you give for your children the best ever. All children love parties, but for us parents it can be a different story. I suspect every mum would be able to relate some horror story concerning a children's party that she has organised. Perhaps after reading and using this book, such disasters will be strictly a thing of the past.

The book is divided into chapters on parties for various age groups, starting with pre-school children. Each section contains advice on general party planning and how to cope with some of the problems that may occur, as well as several suggestions for party themes. Each has its own menu, planned specifically for it; and each menu has plenty of recipes for savouries, cakes and biscuits, as well as a choice of dishes based on Chivers jelly. In the final chapter you will find a selection of games to suit all ages.

There is nothing more rewarding for any parent who has organised a children's party than to see the delighted young faces of children who have thoroughly enjoyed themselves, but it does take hard work and lots of pre-planning. In fact, the secret of any successful party is good planning, whether the party is for a few children at home, or for a larger number in the local village hall.

INITIAL PREPARATION
The first decision to make about the party you are planning is the form it should take, and there are several factors to be considered in this decision, which all relate to each other. The first thing to take into account is the age of the children. Next consider the facilities available at home, as these often control the number to be invited, which also depends upon the cost involved.

A small party held at home is usually best for the very young, with the mothers invited as well. No games need be organised, just provide a selection of toys for the children to play with. For five- and six-year-

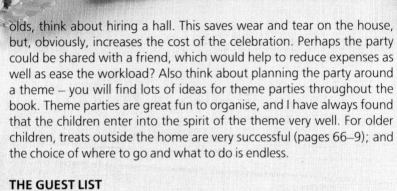

olds, think about hiring a hall. This saves wear and tear on the house, but, obviously, increases the cost of the celebration. Perhaps the party could be shared with a friend, which would help to reduce expenses as well as ease the workload? Also think about planning the party around a theme – you will find lots of ideas for theme parties throughout the book. Theme parties are great fun to organise, and I have always found that the children enter into the spirit of the theme very well. For older children, treats outside the home are very successful (pages 66–9); and the choice of where to go and what to do is endless.

THE GUEST LIST
When selecting the guests, it is best not to mix the age groups too much, as interests change so quickly. I have found that, up to the age

Before the fun begins!

of seven, boys and girls mix very well but, after that age, the great divide seems to start. Talk to your child about who they want: there may be a special new friend that you have missed. If the party is to be held at home, decide upon your ideal number of guests, bearing in mind not only the size of the room where the games are to be held but also the space available for tea. Having children all cramped together while eating can invite disaster. Expect to have to be flexible about numbers. You are sure to have children not turn up who have accepted and others arrive without having replied to the invitation.

THE INVITATIONS

Ideally, send out the invitations about two weeks before the party. If possible, deliver them by hand and make sure the mums of younger

children know that a party is in the offing. It is amazing how easily an invitation can get lost between school and home.

Either buy or make the invitations – you will find ideas for making invitations throughout the book. It can add to the excitement of the occasion if the child whose party it is helps make them. Remember to include all the relevant information on home-made invitations:

- Whose party it is.
- The day and date of the party.
- Where the party is to be held – include a map if the location might prove difficult to find.
- The duration of the party – start time and finish time. For the very young, about one and a half hours is long enough; by the time the children reach the age of seven, arrange for the party to last about two hours; and three-hour parties suit the older children.
- Special instructions, such as fancy dress, swimming gear, old clothes, and so on.
- Where to reply – include not only the address but, if possible, a telephone number as well.

THE FOOD AND DRINK

Choose the food you serve with care, as it is a very important part of the party. Children are never very adventurous when it comes to eating, so stick to the familiar savoury items such as sandwiches, sausages and crisps. With the sweet items you can be a little more bold, and make them as attractive and colourful as possible. However, it is best to avoid giving very rich, creamy or sticky foods to over-excited children.

Make the table as attractive and colourful as possible too, and use paper plates and cups for ease. It is wise to lay a thick layer of paper or a sheet under the tablecloth, or use a plastic tablecloth, so that you can deal with any spills with the minimum of fuss. Arrange each type of food on several small plates, so that the children don't have to stretch across, and to avoid any arguments. I suggest that you put out the sandwiches, sausages, and other savouries first, leaving the cake, biscuits and jellies for when the children are ready for them. Don't fill their drinking cups more than half full each time, to avoid accidents. It might be a good idea to ask the mums of the very young children to bring along beakers with lids, if these are what those children normally use.

An older child will generally eat more than a younger child but, as a rough guide, allow for each child: 4 savoury items; 3 small sweet items; a jelly-type dessert; a piece of birthday cake; 2 cups of drink – about 250 ml (8 fl oz). A litre of concentrated cordial (1¾ pints) makes about 36 diluted drinks.

Sandwiches

There are twenty-two slices in an average loaf of bread, for which you will need about 125 g (4 oz) of softened butter. The following sandwich, roll or vol-au-vent filling recipes are each sufficient to fill six sandwich rounds, top twelve bridge-roll halves or fill twelve small vol-au-vent cases. Add shredded lettuce, sliced tomato and sliced cucumber to decorate the rolls or vol-au-vent cases, if you like.

Egg and cress Mash together 3 hard-boiled eggs, 50 g (2 oz) softened butter and 2 tablespoons of salad cream; mix in a punnet of cress.

Cheese and chives Mix together 125 g (4 oz) grated cheese, 25 g (1 oz) softened butter, a little milk and chopped chives.

Ham and tomato Mix together 125 g (4 oz) minced ham and 1 tablespoon each of tomato ketchup and mayonnaise.

Liver sausage Blend 125 g (4 oz) liver sausage with 50 g (2 oz) cream cheese. Season with a little Worcestershire sauce as required.

Jam Allow 250 g (8 oz) Hartley's pure fruit jam (any flavour) to fill eight sandwich rounds, top twelve sweet bridge-roll halves and fill eight vol-au-vents. Add whipped cream if desired.

Basic recipe: Sponge Cake Mixture

This mixture forms the basis of many of the novelty cakes and other small cakes you will find throughout the book. See your chosen recipe for the right size cookware and cooking times.

> 250 g (8 oz) soft margarine
> 250 g (8 oz) caster sugar
> 4 eggs (size 2)
> 250 g (8 oz) self-raising flour

Put the soft margarine, caster sugar, eggs and flour into a bowl, stir them together, then beat for at least a minute until well blended. The mixture is ready to use when it is light in colour and fluffy in texture.

Flavour variations

Chocolate Substitute 25 g (1 oz) sifted cocoa powder for the same amount of flour.

Orange or lemon Add the grated rind of 1 orange or 1 lemon, plus 2 tablespoons juice.

Coffee Mix in 1 tablespoon coffee essence.

Baking variations

Fairy cakes Half the quantity of the Sponge Cake Mixture makes about eighteen cakes. Bake in paper cases placed in patty tins, so that the cakes keep their shape. Cook at Gas Mark 5/190°C/375°F for about 15 minutes.

Tiny tot cakes A quarter of the Sponge Cake Mixture will make about eighteen cakes. Arrange sweet cases on a baking tray and put 1/2 teaspoon of mixture in each. Bake at Gas Mark 5/190°C/375°F for about 10 minutes.

Basic recipe: Buttercream Mixture

This is the basic recipe for buttercream used throughout the book. See your chosen recipe for variations.

250 g (8 oz) butter
500 g (1 lb) icing sugar, sifted

Beat the butter until it is very soft, then gradually beat in the icing sugar until the buttercream is light in colour and fluffy in texture. Beat in a little warm water if the icing is too stiff, then add flavouring or colouring according to the recipe.

USEFUL TECHNIQUES

To make jelly
Take a jelly and dissolve it in 300 ml (½ pint) hot water; add enough cold water to make 600 ml (1 pint) of liquid. Alternatively, put the jelly block in a jug, add 150 ml (¼ pint) cold water and dissolve the jelly in the microwave on High for 1½ to 2 minutes, stirring after 1 minute; then add enough cold water to make the liquid up to 600 ml (1 pint). To speed up the setting process, add ice cubes instead of water to the dissolved jelly to make the liquid up to 600 ml (1 pint).

To unmould jelly
Have ready the serving dish and a large bowl of fairly hot water. With your fingers, ease the jelly away from the sides of the mould. Immerse the jelly completely in the hot water for about 1 second, dry the mould, and then shake it slightly to loosen the jelly. Moisten the centre of the serving plate so that the jelly can be moved should it not turn out in the centre of the dish. Invert the plate on to the mould and then turn the two the right way up. Shake the mould and plate once, then carefully lift off the mould. Wipe up any excess moisture and serve as soon as possible.

To chop jelly

Make the jelly with 150 ml (¼ pint) less liquid than usual, and leave it to set. Have ready a piece of wet greaseproof paper. Turn out the set jelly on to it, sprinkle with water, then, using a sharp knife, chop the jelly as required.

To melt chocolate

Put the chocolate on a plate over a pan of hot water and allow it to melt slowly, stirring occasionally.

To colour coconut

Put the coconut on a plate, dilute a few drops of food colouring with 1 teaspoon of water and add to the coconut. Using a fork, work together until the coconut is evenly coloured.

PRESENTS AND PRIZES

For going-home presents, and prizes won during the party, collect items such as pencils and notepads, badges, soap bubbles, rubbers, and pencil-tops, as they are very popular with all age-groups. Inexpensive jokes are also much appreciated by the older children. These can all be found in toy shops or stationers, and some shops even sell packs of six small gifts, such as necklaces, which reduces the cost considerably. Provide each child with a party bag (a spare one for an unexpected guest is a good idea). I have found it best to have the bags to hand throughout the games; as a prize is won, it can be put immediately into the right bag, avoiding any panic-stricken searches for lost prizes at the end of the party. Provide lots of balloons so that every child can take one home, with some spare to give to any children accompanying parents when they come to collect a brother or sister.

TO SAVE THE DAY

The following list contains some very general points to bear in mind when planning parties for all age groups. For more specific problems and pitfalls for a particular age group, see the relevant chapter.

- ✔ Remove any special ornaments, and shut off any rooms and areas that are out of bounds.

- ✔ Point out where toilets and washing facilities are, and mark them with a notice.

- ✔ Keep the first-aid kit close at hand; it probably won't be needed, but it is better to be safe than sorry.

- ✔ Enrol as much adult help as possible.

- ✔ Make a list of all the games you have decided to play and make sure you have all the necessary equipment ready for each game long before the party starts.

- ✔ Always have more prizes than you need, plus an extra party bag; some games might have joint winners and unexpected guests may turn up.

- ✔ Spare pants and extra clothes might be needed at parties for younger children. Accidents happen when kids get over-excited.

- ✔ A video of the party is a great memento. Try to find a willing operator.

- ✔ View the day with pleasure; well-planned parties really are great fun!

Parties for under-fives

It isn't really until a child reaches two years of age that birthdays and parties take on any meaning. Even then, many children invited to a party are wary of being left in a strange house with unknown adults, so, for the very young, I think mother-and-toddler parties are best. However, by four years old children should be starting to become independent, and will probably be quite happy for their mothers to leave them at a party.

MOTHER-AND-TODDLER PARTIES
Even when the children are very young and don't quite understand what parties are, it is still fun to celebrate a son or daughter's birthday with either other members of the family or a few toddler friends and their mothers.

Plan the party in the afternoon, ideally after any children who need it have had their afternoon nap. The party should last no more than one to one and a half hours and, although the children will not play organised games, there should be plenty of toys and perhaps some balloons to keep them happy. If your child has one particular toy that is very special, put it away before the party starts, so that it is not a temptation to the other children. It isn't necessary to go to a lot of trouble decorating the room for very young children; safety is really more important. Just have a few balloons about, but do keep an eye on them, as many children are quite frightened when a balloon bursts. Clear the room as much as possible, removing ornaments and precious possessions; your child may know not to touch, but you cannot expect other children to know the same. Also, ensure that there are no loose flexes about. A tape of nursery rhymes creates a pleasant background for the party, and it can also prove very useful should a diversion be needed for an upset child.

The tea
As soon as the guests arrive, I suggest you have tea; if space permits, the kitchen would be the most suitable place. If you have to use the dining-room, it is advisable to cover the floor with a plastic sheet. Let

the children kneel on the chairs rather than perch them on cushions, and don't cram the chairs too close together or squabbles might break out. Have rigid plastic plates and mugs for safety; children at this age still cannot cope with paper or soft plastic.

Keep lots of cloths close at hand in case of spillages. Very young children don't eat vast quantities of food, but often like to have a little of everything, so try and serve a good selection of fairly small items from which they can choose. Check with the mums before the party that none of the children have any particular food dislikes or allergies.

Select five or six items, including the birthday cake and some sort of dessert, from the suggested menu. Place the savoury food on the table first and then, when the children have had enough, add the cakes and biscuits. Too much food on the table at once can confuse children so young, and they will tend to go immediately to the cakes and biscuits rather than the savoury food. Eye appeal is very important, so try and make all the food colourful and attractive. It is simpler to serve just one variety of drink. Only half-fill the mugs each time in case of accidents. Here are a few suggestions for the tea:

MENU UNDER-FIVES PARTIES

Sandwiches Cut into small squares or fingers (see page 7 for filling suggestions)

Party sausages It is not a good idea to put the sausages on to cocktail sticks, so pile them into wooden bowls

Small cheese straws

Tiny tot cakes (page 8), glacé-iced

Chocolate finger biscuits

Jelly Castles (page 20)

The Hickory Dickory Dock Birthday Cake (page 22)

THEME PARTIES FOR UNDER-FIVES

TEDDY BEARS' PICNIC
A marvellous party for the very young, with each guest asked to bring along his or her favourite teddy, so that everyone has a friend.

The invitations
Draw the shape of a teddy bear on some yellow card. If you can't draw it freehand, you should be able to find a reference to trace in a child's book. Cut round the shape, then draw the face, paws and a large bow-tie on one side, writing the party invitation on the other. Don't forget to invite the guests' teddies as well.

The party
As the guests arrive, have the music 'The Teddy Bears' Picnic' playing, and try and keep the teddy bear theme running throughout the party. Games can be adapted, so that, for example, Donkey's Tail (page 94) becomes Teddy's Bow-Tie.

The tea
If the weather is fine, you can have a real picnic tea outside, otherwise you can hold the party indoors; spread a plastic tablecloth on the ground or floor for the guests to sit round. Pack the food and a serviette for each child into individual cake boxes (obtainable from bakers) and put the children's names on them, so that each guest has a food box. The joy of this for the organiser is that most of the crumbs go back into the box; for some reason the children eat most of the food, so clearing up is just a question of gathering up all of the boxes and discarding them. Here are a few suggestions:

MENU TEDDY BEARS PICNIC

Pack into a sandwich box:

Teddy Sandwiches Two small toasted or plain honey
   sandwiches cut into teddy shapes using a biscuit
   cutter (pictured on page 25)

Jelly bear cakes Tiny tot cakes (page 8), glacé-iced
   and decorated with jelly bears

Teddy biscuits Shrewsbury biscuit mixture cut out into
   teddy bears, using a biscuit cutter

Hula hoops (or the equivalent), in a small bag

Drink In a small carton

To be handed round separately:

Teddy Jellies Cut disposable dishes into the shape of a
   teddy bear's head, set Chivers jelly in each, then use
   sweets to give the bear a face

The Teddy Birthday Cake (page 24)

NURSERY RHYME PARTY

Suitable for boys and girls alike, this could be a fancy dress party, if you like. Games are easily arranged around nursery rhymes, one of the most popular for pre-school children being Oranges and Lemons. Here are a few suggestions for tea:

MENU NURSERY RHYME PARTY

Tommy Tucker sandwiches (see page 7 for filling suggestions)

Butterfly bites Small cheese biscuits, each piped with a savoury filling, and topped with the two halves of another cheese biscuit to resemble the wings of a butterfly

Queen of Hearts tarts Jam tarts filled with a variety of Hartley's jams (pictured on page 56/7)

Silver bells Shrewsbury biscuit mixture cut into bell shapes, and decorated with glacé icing and silver balls

Oranges and Lemons (page 27)

Humpty Dumpty cake Use a Battenberg cake as the wall and make a Humpty Dumpty out of paper

The Wishing Well Birthday Cake (page 28)

The Hickory Dickory Dock Birthday Cake (page 22)

The Hickory Dickory Dock Birthday Cake (page 22)

FAIRYLAND PARTY

For this party, make the birthday girl fairy queen for the day, with her own special crown to wear, and throne to sit on at tea.

The invitations

Make invitations in the shape of a fairy wand. If any of the girls have pretty dancing dresses, it might be a fun idea to ask them to come dressed as fairies, and any boys invited could dress up as elves.

The party

Make the party room as pretty as possible, with lots of silver stars cut from tinfoil, pink crêpe paper streamers, and even tinsel. You could also use the Christmas tree lights, placed well out of reach, with no trailing flex. Select some of the games (page 92) that have a fairy theme, such as Witches in the Castle.

The tea

Make the food as dainty as possible. Here are a few suggestions:

MENU FAIRYLAND PARTY

Mini sausage rolls

Bite-size sandwiches (see page 7 for filling suggestions)

Magic meringues Mini pink and white meringues, sandwiched with chocolate spread (pictured on page 20/1)

Fairy Cushions (page 23)

The Fairy Castle Birthday Cake (page 26)

TO SAVE THE DAY

Here are some useful ideas and reminders that could prevent a few mishaps on the day!

☑ Have some disposable nappies and spare pairs of pants to hand in case of accidents.

☑ Ensure that doors to rooms that are not to be used are firmly closed.

☑ Remind mums to bring bibs and covered drinking containers, if still required.

☑ If the party is to be held outside, tell the mums, so that they can dress their children accordingly. Pretty party frocks are not ideal for digging in sandpits.

☑ Be prepared for very young guests not to want to part with the present they have brought. It is sometimes a good idea for the parent to take charge of it.

☑ Opening presents can become very confusing so, if possible, leave them until the guests have departed and there is not so much going on.

☑ Very young children cannot concentrate for long periods, so do provide lots of different activities. Drawing, building bricks, books and wooden toys are all very popular.

☑ Party bags for the very young are not really necessary: a balloon or a lollipop handed out at the end of the party is sufficient.

☑ Don't encourage the children to take a slice of birthday cake home with them: if it is not squashed on the way home it will probably be left in the cake tin to go stale.

See 'To save the day' on page 11 as well; many of the points are relevant to under-fives' parties.

RECIPES

Jelly Castles

Makes 4

1 Chivers jelly, any flavour
300 ml (½ pint) milk
To complete
4 small flags or a few coloured strands

4 × 150 ml (¼ pint) jelly moulds

Dissolve the jelly in 150 ml (¼ pint) hot water and then make the liquid up to 300 ml (½ pint) with cold water. Leave to cool, and, when it is starting to set, stir in the milk. Rinse the moulds in cold water, divide the jelly between them, and then leave to set completely.

Dip the moulds in hot water, turn on to plates and place a flag or a few coloured strands on the top of each.

Magic Meringues (page

Jelly Castles

The Fairy Castle Birthday Cake
(page 26)

Fairy Cushions (page 23)

The Hickory Dickory Dock Birthday Cake

Pictured on page 17
Basic recipes: Sponge Cake Mixture (page 8)
*   Buttercream Mixture (page 9)*

butter, for greasing
half-quantity Sponge Cake Mixture
three-quarters quantity Buttercream Mixture
75 g (3 oz) white marzipan, rolled (optional)
25 g (1 oz) cocoa powder
Smarties
To complete
a small piece of cord, cut in two
a small fluffy chick and a toy mouse

21 cm (8½-inch) round cake tin
a large round or rectangular cake board
a shell and fine nozzle and piping bag

Preheat the oven to Gas Mark 5/190°C/375°F. Grease and base-line the cake tin; then spread the cake mixture in it, and bake the cake for 30 minutes, or until it is golden-brown and well-risen. Turn out on to a wire tray to cool.

To assemble the clock, cut the sponge into a clock shape with a 10 cm (4-inch) base, 14 cm (5½-inch) sloping sides and an 11 cm (4½-inch) sloping roof, or make it more rectangular, as in the photograph. Mark a 10 cm (4-inch) circle in the centre for the clock face. Spread it with about 3 tablespoons of the plain buttercream, or cut out a circle of marzipan and position. Put the cake on to the board. Beat the cocoa powder into the rest of the buttercream and use some to cover the rest of the cake. Mark the sides with a fork and then, with the rest of the icing, pipe a shell edge top and bottom and also outline the clock face. Pipe the numbers around the clock and decorate with the Smarties. Add the hands of the clock, positioned at the age of the child.

Use the spare pieces of cake to make the pendulums. Arrange their cut edges together to make two pendulums. Trim the pieces to match, if necessary, and then place them in position on the board, attached by two lengths of cord. Cover or pipe with icing, then complete the cake with the cuckoo (the chick) and the mouse.

Fairy Cushions

Pictured on page 20/1

Makes about 64

oil, for greasing
2 Chivers lemon jellies
250 g (8 oz) caster sugar
½ teaspoon cream of tartar
1 dessertspoon lemon juice
a pinch of salt
icing sugar, for dusting
cornflour, for dusting

17 cm (7-inch) square cake tin

Lightly oil the cake tin. Put the jellies in a pan with the sugar, cream of tartar and 300 ml (½ pint) water. Gently heat the mixture and, when the jellies and sugar have dissolved, carefully bring the liquid to the boil. It will rise rapidly in the pan as it comes to the boil, so watch it constantly. Boil the mixture rapidly for 5 minutes until it forms a short thread. To test for this, put a small amount on a wooden spoon, dip the tip of your index finger into the liquid, then press it against your thumb. Gradually release your finger and thumb, and, if a short thread is formed, the mixture is ready. Cool until it begins to set, and then add the lemon juice and the salt, and whisk the mixture until it becomes thick and frothy. Pour it into the tin and leave to set.

Turn the set jelly out on to a board lightly dusted with icing sugar and cornflour. Cut the jelly into small pieces. Dust them with icing sugar and cornflour, then pile the fairy cushions into dishes to serve.

The Teddy Birthday Cake

Basic recipes: Sponge Cake Mixture (page 8)
Buttercream Mixture (page 9)

butter, for greasing
1 quantity Sponge Cake Mixture
1 quantity Buttercream Mixture
brown and yellow food colouring
Smarties
liquorice comfits (optional)
To complete
a card, ribbon or liquorice bow-tie

16 cm (6½-inch) and 18 cm (7½-inch) round cake tins
4 empty 200 g baked bean cans
a number 8 star nozzle and piping bag
35 cm (14-inch) round or 46 × 58 cm (21 × 18-inch) rectangular
   cake board

Preheat the oven to Gas Mark 5/190°C/375°F. Grease and base-line all
the tins; then divide the sponge mixture between them, filling the
baked bean cans less than half full. The small cakes will take about
15 minutes to bake, the larger ones between 20 and 30 minutes.
When they are cooked, turn them out on to a wire tray to cool.

Beat enough yellow colouring into the buttercream to make a good
colour. On the board, position the largest sponge as the bear's body,
using the smaller sponge· for its head. Cut a sliver off each sponge
where they meet, so that they fit together neatly. Using one of the
baked bean cans, cut out 4 arcs in the body of the bear, and position
the small cakes for paws. Use two of these arcs for ears, and the other
two, cut into shape, for the bear's nose. Spread the cake with a thin
layer of buttercream. Spoon about half of the remaining buttercream
into the piping bag with the nozzle attached, and pipe stars over the
bear's ears, nose and paws. Leaving about 2 tablespoons for the final
decoration, spread the remaining buttercream until the bear is
completely covered, apart from two oval-shaped spaces on either side

The Teddy Birthday Cake Teddy Sandwiches (page 15)

of the nose for the eyes. Fork a fur-like pattern on to the body. Colour the remaining buttercream dark brown, spoon it into the icing bag and fill in the eye spaces. Put a Smartie or a liquorice comfit for a pupil on each, and use another two Smarties for the nose.

Use either the brown icing or more Smarties for the buttons, and then position the bow-tie. If you want candles on the cake, you could put them in candle-holders in the button positions.

The Fairy Castle Birthday Cake

Pictured on page 20/1
Basic recipe: Buttercream Mixture (page 9)

pink food colouring
1 quantity Buttercream Mixture
4 jam-filled swiss rolls
To complete
4 paper doilies
white paper
kitchen foil
cocktail sticks
To decorate
foil flags on cocktail sticks (optional)
coloured strands

a number 6 star nozzle and piping bag
25 cm (10-inch) round cake board

Beat a few drops of colouring into the buttercream until it becomes a pretty shade of pink, and then spread a thin layer over the board.

Cut a 5 cm (2-inch) slice off one of the swiss rolls and, using some buttercream, stick it to the end of another swiss roll. The castle is formed by grouping together four up-ended swiss roll pieces: position the extra-tall swiss roll on end on the board first. Put a normal-size swiss roll just touching it at the back on one side, with the slightly smaller swiss roll opposite at the front. Cut the last swiss roll in half and position one piece right at the front, between the other two towers (you will have half a swiss roll spare, but I'm sure it will be eaten).

Spread the castle completely with the buttercream, using a knife point to draw a brick effect. Darken the rest of the icing with a little more pink colouring, put it into the piping bag with nozzle attached and pipe in the door and windows.

Cut each doily in half, and cut out a piece of white paper a little smaller. Shape each into a cone just a little larger than the diameter of each tower and secure with sellotape. Line each doily cone with a white paper cone and put one on each tower. If you like, cut foil flags, stick them to cocktail sticks and carefully place one in the top of each cone. To complete the fairy castle, sprinkle coloured strands all over the cake board.

Oranges and Lemons

Pictured on page 4/5

Makes 16 pieces

4 large oranges
1 Chivers lemon jelly

Make up the jelly, using 300 ml (½ pint) water, and leave on one side. Cut each orange in half through the stalk and scoop out the flesh. Discard as much as possible of the membranes around the orange segments, and then chop or blend the fruit. Put it on one side. Clean the orange shells well, removing as much of the pith as possible. Put the shells on a plate.

When the jelly has almost set, make it up to 600 ml (1 pint) with the fruit. Divide the mixture beween the orange shells and leave them in a cool place overnight to set completely.

Next day, cut each shell in half and serve the wedges on a large plate – the children will adore them.

The Wishing Well Birthday Cake

a little Hartley's jam, plus extra for the roof
1 packet of sponge fingers
4 trifle sponge cakes
385 g (13 oz) can of Hartley's strawberries in syrup
1 Chivers strawberry jelly
2 eggs
To complete
1 metre × 1 cm (39 × ½-inch) dark pink ribbon
2 large chocolate flake bars
12 × 15 cm (5 × 6-inch) piece of stiff card
chocolate buttons, for the tiles
jelly sweets

17 cm (6½-inch) round loose-based cake tin
20 cm (8-inch) round cake board

Spread a little jam along the side of each sponge finger, and then position them on end around the side of the tin, trimming them where necessary. Split the sponge cakes in half, spread with jam and sandwich together. Place the cakes in the bottom of the tin, trimming them to fit. Drain the strawberries, pouring the syrup over the sponge cakes in the base of the tin. Blend the strawberries to a purée.

Break the jelly into squares, put it in a pan with 150 ml (¼ pint) water and dissolve over a low heat. Stir into the strawberry purée.

Separate the eggs and beat the yolks into the fruit mixture. Whisk the egg whites until they are stiff, and then, using a metal spoon, fold them lightly and quickly into the fruit mixture as it begins to set. Pour the mixture into the lined cake tin and leave overnight to set.

Next day, remove the dessert from the tin and place it on the cake board. Encircle the sides twice with ribbon and push the two flakes in on either side for roof supports. Fold the stiff card in half to make a roof 15 × 6 cm (6 × 2½ inches). Spread the roof with jam and carefully 'tile' it by sticking the chocolate buttons onto the jam. Gently place the roof on top of the flakes. Pile the small jelly sweets into the centre of the well.

Parties for 5 & 6-year-olds

By this age, children are starting to have fairly clear ideas about what they like and dislike, so most probably will want to get involved in the organisation of their own parties. I think this makes the planning much more fun. Discuss with them the type of party they want, but do start with a few very clear ideas in your head as to what you feel would be suitable. You may feel it would be wiser to hire a hall, if finances permit, as that saves a lot of wear and tear on the house and provides a clear area in which the children can play, so there is a greater variety of suitable games. The more children at the party, the more adult help will be required. As a rough guide, I would advise you to have at least one adult to every five children.

Let your child decide on the guest list, with a little help and guidance. Again, if finances permit, hiring an entertainer can save a lot of headaches; he will amuse the children for the duration of the party, with, perhaps, magic tricks, party games or even puppet or animal shows. Since entertainers can be quite expensive, you might consider arranging a joint birthday party. If no one can recommend an entertainer, try looking in the Yellow Pages. You will have to plan well ahead, as most are booked up weeks in advance.

The food
Plan a menu that is fairly basic but with a varied selection. Popular items at this age are crisps, small sausages, pieces of cheese, chunks of pineapple and even pieces of carrot. Avoid any rich and sticky cakes, but you will find that biscuits such as shortbread are very welcome. If there are going to be quite a few children at the party, it is best to arrange a small plate of the main items of food for each guest, to include four savoury items and two sweet. Then place the crisps and so on in small bowls down the centre of the table, so that the children can help themselves. Bring the jelly dessert out towards the end of the tea, and, finally, place the birthday cake in the centre of the table for the birthday child to blow out the candles and have everyone sing 'Happy Birthday'. But before you give every child a slice of cake, make sure they really want it, as many children will be too full.

THEME PARTIES FOR 5 & 6-YEAR-OLDS

ANIMAL CIRCUS PARTY

The invitations
An elephant shape cut from pink card would make a fun invitation. Ask the guests either to wear a circus mask or to come dressed as a clown.

The party
Decorate the party room with animal pictures and clown faces and then organise lots of animal games such as 'The Farmer's in his Den' and 'Old MacDonald Had a Farm' – you will find other suggestions on pages 92–5. Before the party, record some songs so that the children can sing along.

The tea
Designate each child's place at the table with an animal biscuit with the child's name piped on it. Arrange the rest of the food on several small plates, so that every child can reach easily. Here are a few suggestions:

MENU ANIMAL CIRCUS PARTY

Spiky hedgehog (pictured on page 4/5) Cheese and pineapple cubes stuck into a foil-covered potato

Cheese straw snakes   Cheese pastry brushed with Marmite, cut into strips and baked

Savoury centipede   A small french stick, split (but not cut through) and filled with egg and cress, with small cocktail sausages for legs, held in place with cocktail sticks, and stuffed olives for eyes

Cheesecake Roundabout   (page 40)

Jelly Clowns   (page 39)

The Pink Elephant Birthday Cake   (page 42)

PIRATE PARTY

The invitations
Cut pirates' hats out of black card and, with a silver felt-tipped pen, draw the 'Jolly Roger' on one side.

The party
Fly the 'Jolly Roger' outside the house instead of the conventional balloons. Guests will probably come in pirate attire, but it might be a good idea to have a few pirate hats and eye patches at hand in case some don't. Organise a treasure hunt in the garden, if weather permits. Another game that boys especially love to play is Tug of War. If you have a large sand-pit, have a treasure hunt. Why not, for this particular party, have a lucky dip at the end?

The food
Arrange the food, if possible, on a low table, so that the children have to kneel or sit cross-legged to eat — this position somehow gives you more control over them! If you don't want to follow the menu below, why not give them fish fingers and chips (oven chips are easiest), then go on to the dessert and cakes as suggested below.

MENU PIRATE PARTY

Sailing boats Bridge-roll halves, topped with a sandwich filling (page 7). Use a triangular slice of cheese for a sail, and attach it with a cocktail stick

Sausage spirals Thin strips of pastry wrapped round uncooked sausages, and baked as sausage rolls; serve with tomato ketchup, if liked

Chocolate cannonballs Very small chocolate truffles (pictured on page 45)

Secret Pools (page 46)

The Galleon Birthday Cake (page 44)

WOODLAND FOLK PARTY

Children tend to be interested in nature and the wildlife of the fields and hedgerows, so this would make a delightful theme for a party for either girls or boys. If possible, hold the party outside and organise games such as a Nature Trail; in this, everyone is given a list of about ten items that they have to find: an oak leaf, a daisy, and so on. The first to collect all the items correctly wins. Here are a few suggestions for tea:

MENU WOODLAND FOLK PARTY

Birds' nests, savoury Vol-au-vent cases with sandwich fillings (page 7), with 2–3 large peanuts for eggs (pictured opposite)

Birds' nests, sweet Vol-au-vent cases filled with Chivers Fruit for-all, topped with whipped cream and small confectionery eggs (pictured opposite)

Squirrels' hoard Small balls of sausagemeat, rolled in dry sage and onion stuffing mix, baked, then served piled into bowls

Badger buns Fairy cakes (page 8) iced in brown and white buttercream (page 9) for the badger's head, with Smarties for the nose and eyes

Jelly Mice (page 38)

Rupert Rabbit (page 47)

The Holly Hedgehog Birthday Cake (page 43)

Rupert Rabbit (page 47)   The Holly Hedgehog Birthday Cake (page 43)
Birds' Nests, sweet and savoury

STAR TREK PARTY

Space travel and the worlds beyond the stars hold a tremendous fascination for young children, so I am sure a space party, especially for the boys, would be much appreciated. The invitations could be spaceship-shaped, and the walls and windows of the party room decorated with planets, moons and stars. Select or adapt games to fit in with the space theme. If possible, provide a space cartoon video for the children to watch quietly after the meal. Here are a few suggestions for tea:

MENU STAR TREK PARTY

Flying saucers Small beefburgers in buns with cocktail-stick aerials, each topped with a small stick of cucumber and a ring of carrot

Guided missiles Small sausages wrapped in bread, fastened with a cocktail stick, deep-fat-fried, and served with tomato ketchup

Moon biscuits Shortbread cut in moon shapes and, if you wish, decorated with icing and silver balls (pictured on page 37)

Black Hole Whip (page 38)

The Space Rocket Birthday Cake (page 36)

TO SAVE THE DAY

✔ Have plenty of games organised, following quickly on from each other, or the children may become restive.

✔ Often you will find that it is the birthday child who is the one who plays up, throwing tantrums and being thoroughly difficult. If this does happen, try and involve him or her in the organisation of the games. After all, one expects plenty of attention at one's own party!

✔ Collect together all the paraphernalia for the games long before the party starts. If you are planning to play Pass the Parcel (page 92), remember to have ready all the necessary items for the forfeits, if included.

✔ Never force children to participate in a game if they don't want to. Invariably, once they see their friends having fun, they change their minds.

✔ If playing a game from which players drop out, have a playboard and chalk or some pens and paper at hand, to occupy those who are no longer playing.

✔ Mark the toilets clearly and put out a few clean towels.

✔ If there are a lot of guests, leave present-opening until after the party, or it will become completely confused, and you will lose track of who sent what.

✔ Don't forget to organise supper for the hungry helpers after the guests have left and the birthday-child is in bed. Also, refreshments during the party, such as tea or perhaps something stronger, are essential.

✔ Excited children can have accidents, so be prepared with a few spare sets of pants.

See also 'To save the day' on page 11; many of the points are also relevant to this age group.

RECIPES

The Space Rocket Birthday Cake

Basic recipes: Sponge Cake Mixture (page 8)
Buttercream Mixture (page 9)

butter, for greasing
two-thirds-quantity Sponge Cake Mixture
grated rind and juice of 1 orange
1 quantity Buttercream Mixture
25 g (1 oz) cocoa powder, sifted
1 jam-filled swiss roll
4 tablespoons Hartley's apricot jam
small colourful sweets
To complete
cardboard and foil
5 sparklers
toy spacemen (optional)

19 cm (7½-inch) square cake tin
25 cm (10-inch) cake board

Preheat the oven to Gas Mark 4/180°C/350°F, and grease and base-line the tin. Make up the Sponge Cake Mixture, adding the orange rind and juice with the rest of the ingredients. Turn the mixture into the tin, spread it to the sides and leave the centre slightly hollow. Bake the cake for about 45 minutes, or until it is springy to the touch. Turn the cake out on to a wire tray to cool.

Divide the buttercream in two, and beat the cocoa powder into one portion. Cut the cake in half horizontally, spread it with jam and sandwich the two pieces back together. Place the cake on the board, and spread the entire surface with the chocolate buttercream. Cut two opposite corners off the cake, to make two triangles, each about 5 cm (2 inches) along their shorter sides, then spread the cut surfaces with more buttercream. Carefully spread the swiss roll with the white

Moon Biscuits (page 34) Black Hole Whip (page 38) The Space Rocket Birthday Cake

buttercream, and position it at an angle on top of the cake, resting on the cut-off corners. Make a nose cap and three fins for the rocket out of the foil-covered cardboard; then place them in position. Decorate the rocket with the sweets, place sparklers in the tail, and then complete the scene with the spacemen, if you wish. When the birthday cake is served, light the sparklers to give the effect of a working rocket.

Black Hole Whip

Serves 6

285 g (10 oz) can of Hartley's blackcurrants
1 Chivers blackcurrant jelly
1 small can of evaporated milk, chilled

750 ml (1¼-pint) jelly mould

Drain the blackcurrants and melt the jelly in the liquid. Make it up to 300 ml (½ pint) with cold water. Pour half this liquid into the jelly mould and leave to set. Keep the rest of the jelly on one side until it is just starting to thicken. Whisk the evaporated milk until it is thick and creamy, and then whisk into the thickening jelly. Carefully fold in the blackcurrants and pour the mixture into the mould, on top of the set jelly. Leave in a cold place overnight to set completely.

Next day, dip the mould into hot water and turn it out on to a plate. Serve with single cream, if you like.

Jelly Mice

Serves 8

1 Chivers lime jelly
875 g can of pear halves
1 glacé cherry
currants
liquorice bootlaces

Dissolve the jelly in 150 ml (¼ pint) boiling water. Drain the pear halves and add the liquid to the jelly, making it up to 450 ml (¾ pint) with extra cold water if necessary. Pour the jelly into a shallow dish and leave to set.

Turn the jelly on to wet greaseproof paper, and chop it (page 10). Spoon it on to a flat plate. Position the pear halves on top of the jelly and add two currants for eyes, a small piece of glacé cherry for a nose and a length of bootlace for the tail.

Jelly Clowns

Pictured on page 41

Makes 6

>1 Chivers raspberry or orange jelly
>1 small packet of dessert topping
>colourful sweets (optional)
>glacé cherries (optional)
>
>6 china egg cups
>a small nozzle and piping bag

Make up the jelly to 450 ml (¾ pint), and pour half into the egg cups. Leave in a cool place to set. Wet a piece of greaseproof paper and put it on a plate, dip the set jellies into hot water and unmould each on to the damp paper. Fill the egg cups with the rest of the jelly and leave in a cool place.

When the jelly in the egg cups has set, carefully slip the first set of jelly eggs on top, so that the flat sides are together, to form the heads of the clowns. Make up the dessert topping, and, with the nozzle, pipe crosses for the clown's eyes, a ruffle, and some hair. Use slices of glacé cherries for their mouths, if you like. You can also use bits of sweets, stuck on with the dessert topping, for their eyes, and even for whoopie whistles!

Cheesecake Roundabout

Serves 8–10

For the base
50 g (2 oz) margarine
125 g (4 oz) digestive biscuits, crushed
25 g (1 oz) caster sugar
For the filling
325 g (11 oz) can of mandarin pieces
1 Chivers orange jelly
250 g (8 oz) curd cheese
150 ml (¼ pint) double cream, whipped
To decorate
16 animal biscuits
Hartley's apricot jam
To complete
a 15 cm (6-inch) cardboard tube, covered in foil
a circular piece of pretty card 20 cm (8 inches) in diameter,
for the canopy

20 cm (8-inch) spring-clip cake tin
23 cm (9-inch) cake board

Melt the margarine, stir in the biscuits and sugar and turn the mixture into the tin. Spread level.

Drain the fruit, reserving the liquid. Make up the fruit juice to 300 ml (½ pint) with hot water and dissolve the jelly in it. Leave to cool. Beat the cheese until soft. When the jelly is starting to set, gradually beat in the cheese and the fruit. Fold in the whipped cream and then pour the mixture on to the base and leave to set.

When it has set, release the cheesecake from the tin and put on a plate or cake board. Using the jam to attach them, evenly space the animal biscuits around the side of the cheesecake. Stand the foil-covered tube in the centre of the cake. Cut into the centre of the piece of card, overlap the edges to form a cone shape, then stick down. Put the canopy on the foil-covered tube.

Jelly Clowns (page 39) Cheesecake Roundabout

The Pink Elephant Birthday Cake

Pictured on front cover
Basic recipes: Sponge Cake Mixture (page 8)
*   Buttercream Mixture (page 9)*

butter, for greasing
1 quantity Sponge Cake Mixture
Hartley's raspberry jam
1 quantity Buttercream Mixture
pink food colouring
dolly mixtures
liquorice comfits
To complete
fan-shaped piece of card covered with foil, or 75 g (3 oz) white
    marzipan, for the ear

20 cm (8-inch) round cake tin
25 cm (10-inch) round or 25 × 27 cm (10 × 11-inch) rectangular
    cake board
a small star nozzle and piping bag

Grease and base-line the tin. Preheat the oven to Gas Mark 4/180°C/
350°F. Put the cake mixture into the tin, spread it to the sides, leaving
the centre slightly hollow, and then bake for 45–50 minutes, until
golden-brown and shrinking away from the sides of the tin. Turn out
on to a wire tray to cool.

Cut the cake in half horizontally, spread it with jam and sandwich it
back together again. Cut out a circle of greaseproof paper the size of
the cake, to be used as a template.

Draw a line 16 cm (6½ inches) across the paper, from edge to edge,
and then place a 16 cm (6½-inch) tin in the centre of the line, flush
with the edge of the circle, and draw round it. Cut these pieces out,
and then place the larger pieces of the template on the cake and cut
them out. Trim the tips off the larger piece of the cake to make the two
flat feet of the animal, and place the main cake on the board.

From the smaller piece of cake, cut out an 8 cm (3-inch) circle for the
head; then shape the other pieces for the trunk and a small tail. Cut

out a small arc in the body piece, so the head fits neatly, then put all remaining pieces in position on the board.

Beat enough pink colouring into the buttercream to make a fairly strong colour. Spread the entire cake with a thin layer, and then put some more buttercream into the bag, with the star nozzle, and pipe stars all over the main cake, the head, trunk, legs and tail. Complete the elephant with liquorice comfits and dolly mixtures. Finally, put the foil-covered piece of card, if using, in place for the ear, or colour the marzipan pink, mould the ear and put it in position.

The Holly Hedgehog Birthday Cake

Pictured on page 33
Basic recipes: Sponge Cake Mixture (page 8)
Buttercream Mixture (page 9)

butter, for greasing
three-quarters-quantity Sponge Cake Mixture
1 tablespoon coffee essence
1 tablespoon milk
To decorate
half-quantity Buttercream Mixture
3 tablespoons coffee esssence
3 Smarties
125 g (4 oz) chocolate buttons

21 cm (8½-inch) round cake tin

Preheat the oven to Gas Mark 4/180°C/350°F. Grease and base-line the tin.

Make up the cake mixture, folding in the coffee essence and milk after the flour. Turn the mixture into the cake tin, and spread it to the sides, hollowing out the centre slightly. Bake the cake on the centre shelf for 45 minutes, or until it feels springy to the touch, and is slightly shrinking away from the sides of the tin. Turn out on to a wire tray to cool.

Make the buttercream, flavouring it with the coffee essence. Spread a little buttercream over the base of the cake, cut it into two semicircles, and sandwich the two semi-circular surfaces together. Stand the cake on the cut surface to give the hedgehog the rounded shape. To complete the shape, with a sharp knife cut out a curved piece 6 cm (2½ inches) from one edge for the snout, then trim a wedge off either side of this for the pointed nose. Cover the entire cake with butter-cream and carefully lift it on to a plate, then rough the surface with a fork. Place the Smarties in position for eyes and a nose, with two whole chocolate buttons for ears. Finally, to make the spines, cut the remaining buttons in half and press them into the buttercream all over the hedgehog.

The Galleon Birthday Cake

Basic recipes: Sponge Cake Mixture (page 8)
Buttercream Mixture (page 9)

butter, for greasing
1 quantity Sponge Cake Mixture
Hartley's apricot jam
1 quantity Buttercream Mixture
red food colouring
1 tablespoon cocoa powder
some short Matchmakers, for the rails
1 Chivers lemon jelly, made with only 450 ml (¾ pint) water, coloured blue and set
To complete
thin garden canes or straws, for masts
white paper, for sails

2 × 1 kg (2 lb) loaf tins
a small nozzle and piping bag
25 cm (10-inch) square cake board

Preheat the oven to Gas Mark 4/180°C/350°F, and grease and base-line the loaf tins. Divide the cake mixture between them, and bake for 45 minutes, or until golden-brown and springy to the touch. Leave to cool.

Cut each cake through horizontally, spread with jam and re-assemble. Cut one cake vertically in two and the other into three. Sandwich the

Secret Pools (page 46)   The Galleon Birthday Cake

middle third piece of cake beween the two halves of the first cake with jam, to make the base of the boat. Stick one of the outer thirds of cake on top at the stern (rear) of the boat with jam. Separate the final third into two layers and stick one layer next to the raised poop at the stern end, and stick the other piece on the bow. Cut a slight point for the bow, if you wish, and round the other end for the stern.

Colour two-thirds of the buttercream red; beat the cocoa powder into 3 tablespoons of the remainder. Stand the cake on the board. Spread the plain icing over the decks of the boat; the red icing is for the sides of the boat with the chocolate icing at the bottom, if you wish. Use a palette knife to mark the sides of the boat in lines to resemble planks. Cut the Matchmakers in half and stand them around the edge of the decks for the boat railings and, with the nozzle and chocolate icing, pipe a rope to connect them together. Make the rectangular sails using the canes or straws and white paper, and place them in position. You could write a birthday message on one of the sails. Finally, chop the jelly (page 10) and spoon it around the cake for the sea.

Secret Pools

Pictured on page 45

Makes 8

1 Chivers lemon jelly
blue food colouring
8 meringue nests
300 g (10 oz) Chivers apricot Fruit for-all

Make up the jelly to 450 ml (¾ pint), colour it blue and then leave in a shallow bowl to set.

Arrange the meringue nests on a large plate and divide the Fruit for-all between them. Chop the jelly (page 10) and spoon over the fruit filling. Keep in a cool place until required. Serve within an hour of making them, or the meringue may go soft.

Rupert Rabbit

Pictured on page 33

Serves 6

oil, for greasing
1 Chivers orange jelly
2 level tablespoons custard powder
300 ml (½ pint) milk
1 Chivers lime jelly
a few long strips of angelica, for whiskers (optional)

600 ml (1-pint) rabbit jelly-mould

Lightly oil the mould. Melt the orange jelly in 150 ml (¼ pint) hot water. Mix the custard powder to a smooth paste with a little of the milk. Stir in the rest of the milk and heat, stirring all the time, to bring the custard to the boil. Simmer for 1 minute, until it thickens. Stir the jelly into the custard and, when it is well blended, pour the liquid into the mould. Stand it on a plate and leave in a cool place overnight to set. Meanwhile, make up the lime jelly using only 450 ml (¾ pint) of water, and leave it to set.

Next day, dip the rabbit mould quickly into hot water and turn the jelly out on to a plate. Position the angelica strips for whiskers, and then chop the lime jelly (page 10) and spoon it around the mould for grass.

Parties for 7 & 8-year-olds

As children get older, they start to prefer parties that do not follow the traditional lines of tea and games; probably a party for a seven- or eight-year-old will be the last conventional party you will organise.

Children of this age should be able to assist you in planning. They can write out the invitations, and you can all have great fun decorating the party room.

Selecting the party games is another area in which the children could help. The choice of games is that much greater, now that everyone can read and write. Favourites with children of this age are Kim's Game, Advertisements (pages 92–5) and Consequences. Incidentally, Advertisements is ideal for while you are waiting for everyone to arrive. Team games are also very popular with children of this age. Divide them into teams of three or four for the first game and keep to those teams for the whole party. Don't make the teams too large, or the games may last too long, with the children becoming bored and restive. Give each team some sort of identification, such as coloured badges, so the children instantly know who they are playing with. It is a good idea to award just one overall team prize at the end of the party, and for this you need to keep a tally of the teams' scores throughout. Do make sure the scoring is correct, otherwise you could find yourself with a few disgruntled children at the end of the day.

FOOD IN GENERAL
The appearance of food is still very important to children of this age, but they are now starting to become a little more adventurous. I suggest you serve more savoury than sweet items, but make the pieces small enough for the children to be able to sample all the dishes. Straightforward sandwiches are considered by this age-group to be 'boring', so try sandwich kebabs (page 51). Chicken drumsticks, pieces of pizza and sausage rolls are other popular savoury ideas. Allow five savoury items per child, with a choice of cakes and biscuits. Then complete the tea with an individual dessert, and the birthday cake.

Fizzy drinks can be served, and it is sometimes easier to give each

Rock Pools (page 50) Savoury Boats (page 50) Tropical Cream (page 62)

child a can of drink. Limit the choice to just two, otherwise things get out of hand. Allow one can per child and have a few extra in case it's a hot day and the children get very thirsty.

THEME PARTIES FOR 7 & 8-YEAR-OLDS

SHIPWRECK PARTY

The fun of this party is that all the guests are asked to arrive wearing the clothes they were in when they opened their invitation. With luck, some of the guests will come in their pyjamas, to add to the fun; others may come in castaway attire. Plan all the games with a nautical feel. For example, Musical Islands would be ideal (page 93). Party prizes can include shell-shaped chocolates and pink shrimp sweets. Here are a few suggestions for the tea:

MENU SHIPWRECK PARTY

Savoury boats Cheese pastry boats filled with a quiche mixture and baked (pictured on page 49)

Fish on a stick Grilled fish fingers cut in half and served on cocktail sticks, with tomato ketchup

Life belts Ring doughnuts

Rock Pools Set lime jellies in individual dishes, then make fish with canned peach pieces; use currants for their eyes and Polo mints as bubbles (pictured on page 49)

Tropical Cream (page 62)

The Galleon Birthday Cake (page 44)

The Desert Island Birthday Cake (page 60)

MAD HATTER'S TEA PARTY

The invitations
A hat shape would be the obvious choice, cut from colourful card. Ask the guests to come in a mad hat, the best of which will be awarded a prize.

The party
The party should last about two and a half hours. After the first game, put the hats in a safe place so that they aren't damaged. Play games for about 30 minutes before tea, followed immediately by the hat judging. Let the children parade with their hats and award several prizes, for the prettiest hat, the most original, the most colourful, and so on. It is more fun if you encourage all the guests to participate in the voting.

The tea
Make the tea-table as pretty as possible, with perhaps a flower laid beside each place (the birthday-child can decide where everyone is to sit before the party starts). Choose food that looks pretty. Here are a few suggestions:

MENU MAD HATTER'S TEA PARTY

Sandwich kebabs Small squares of filled sandwiches threaded with pieces of raw carrot or red or green pepper or grapes on to cocktail sticks and stuck into a base, such as a grapefruit (pictured on page 56/7)

Cheese scones Split and filled

Queen of Hearts tarts A selection of heart-shaped tarts filled with Hartley's jam (pictured on page 56/7)

Dormouse Delight (page 56)

The Mad Hatter's Hat Birthday Cake (page 63)

SAFARI PARTY

This theme works especially well if the weather is fine and the party can be held outside. You could set up a coconut shy or build an obstacle course in the garden, with ropes, netting and so on, so the children can release some of their energy. Barbecue some of the food before the party starts, if that is easier. Here are a few suggestions for the tea:

MENU SAFARI PARTY

Chicken drumsticks Allow one per child with a few extra

Sesame seed bites Cheese pastry squares, brushed with egg and sprinkled with sesame seeds before baking

Cucumber cobra A cucumber spiked with cheese and pineapple chunks or small pieces of sausage on cocktail sticks (pictured opposite)

Biscuit shields Biscuit mixture cut into shield shapes, baked and decorated with icing and silver balls

Zebra Desserts (page 59)

The Charlie Crocodile Birthday Cake (page 58)

Zebra Desserts (page 59) Cucumber Cobra
The Charlie Crocodile Birthday Cake (page 58)

WILD WEST PARTY

Cowboys and Indians are the theme of this party – ideal for boys, but there is no reason why girls can't join in as well. If you decide on fancy dress, a simple outfit for cowboys or cowgirls is jeans and a checked shirt; for Indians, try a strip of corrugated paper with a feather in it, for the head-dress, and trousers decorated with ribbon or braid.

The invitations

There is a choice of several designs for home-made invitations to a Wild West party, for example, a horse, cut from brown card, or a wigwam, attractively decorated on one side, and with the party invitation, including any fancy dress details, on the other.

The party

If you are feeling adventurous, why not make a totem pole for the party room? Paint several long thin boxes different colours, some with faces on them and others plain. Stick all the boxes one on top of another to form a pole. Make sure that the base is quite sturdy, so that the pole doesn't topple over during the activities.

This theme is perfect for a party held outdoors, especially if you have a tent available, in case it rains in the middle of the fun. No doubt many of the guests will bring toy guns and rifles. Allow the children to keep these during the first game, then store them in a safe place until later. Excited children and toy guns sometimes don't mix too well. It can be pleasant to end an outdoors party with a bonfire and sing-song around it, with parents joining in, perhaps, when they arrive to collect their children.

The tea

As a change from the normal party food, you could serve a hot meal for this particular party – much easier to prepare than making lots of sandwiches and savouries. If you have several adult helpers and the weather is good, the sausages could be cooked on a barbecue, but do place the fire away from where the children are playing, to avoid any accidents. Serve the food on paper plates to save on washing up.

There are several suitable hot dishes from which you can choose (don't forget the tomato ketchup), followed by a selection of cakes and desserts. Here are a few suggestions:

MENU WILD WEST PARTY

Sausages or beefburgers and baked beans Allow about 2 chipolata sausages or 1 beefburger each, with a 425 g (15 oz) can of baked beans between 5

Jacket potatoes Bake 1 potato per child and serve with a choice of butter and grated cheese or baked beans

Indian wigwams Coconut pyramids (pictured on page 65)

The Fort Birthday Cake (page 64)

TO SAVE THE DAY

- ✔ Always organise more games than you think will fit into the time – much better than running out of ideas.

- ✔ Never ask the children what games they want to play, as this only leads to a lot of disagreement.

- ✔ Have someone available to open the door and show the children where to hang their coats. The party can get off to a bad start if there is only one person to open the door and organise the guests who have already arrived.

- ✔ Point out or mark where the toilets are.

- ✔ If you have a video player, have a suitable tape available, in case they all become over-excited.

- ✔ A whistle is very useful to attract the attention of the children when you can't hear yourself speak.

See also 'To save the day' on page 11.

RECIPES

Dormouse Delight

Makes 6

300 g (10 oz) Chivers morello cherry Fruit for-all
150 ml (¼ pint) double cream
4 meringue shells, crushed
50 g (2 oz) grated chocolate
25 g (1 oz) icing sugar, sifted
150 ml (¼ pint) natural yogurt
3 chocolate flake bars

Divide the Fruit for-all between 6 tall glasses. Whip the cream until it is stiff, fold in the crushed meringues, chocolate, icing sugar and yogurt. Spoon the mixture on top of the cherries and complete the dessert with half a flake pushed into each serving.

Dormouse Delight

Queen of Hearts Tarts (page 51)

Sandwich Kebabs (page 51)

The Mad Hatter's Hat Birthday Cake (page 63)

The Charlie Crocodile Birthday Cake

Pictured on page 53
Basic recipes: Sponge Cake Mixture (page 8)
                Buttercream Mixture (page 9)

butter, for greasing
1 quantity Sponge Cake Mixture
1 Chivers lime jelly
4 tablespoons Hartley's raspberry jam
1 quantity Buttercream Mixture
pink, green and blue food colouring
25 g (1 oz) blanched almonds
liquorice allsorts

20 cm (8-inch) square cake tin
30 cm (12-inch) square cake board
a number 8 star nozzle and piping bag

Preheat the oven to Gas Mark 4/180°C/350°F. Grease the tin and line the base with greaseproof paper. Turn the cake mixture into the tin, spread it to the sides and hollow out the centre slightly. Bake for 45–50 minutes. Turn the cake out on to a wire tray to cool.

Make up the jelly, using only 450 ml (¾ pint) water, and leave to set in a shallow container.

Cut the cake in half vertically, to make two equal pieces. One piece is for the crocodile's body – this can be set aside while you make the other piece into the snout and tail. To make the snout, cut out a long triangle from the centre of the piece, making diagonal cuts from the middle of one of its short sides. The large triangle will form the snout of the crocodile, and the other two pieces put together form the long tail. Trim 5 cm (2 inches) off the snout tip, and set aside. To make the feet, cut a 6 cm (2½-inch) strip off the widest part of the tail; this will give you two almost square pieces. Cut each in half diagonally, and place two on each side of the body.

Slice the cake through horizontally, including the mouth piece, spread the body and tail sections with jam, and sandwich back together. Do not jam the mouth piece. Put the body and tail in position on the board. Colour a little of the buttercream pink and spread it over the inside of the mouth piece; put the base of the mouth in position. Cut the small piece of cake from the snout into a wedge shape and place it in the mouth to keep the jaws open. Spread this piece with pink buttercream if possible. Cut the almonds into strips and arrange them around the bottom and top jaw of the crocodile for teeth. Position the top jaw securely (you may need to support the top jaw with a small piece of cardboard), so that the mouth is open to reveal the teeth.

Colour the rest of the buttercream green and, using the piping nozzle and bag, cover the entire surface with small stars. Use the liquorice allsorts for eyes and nostrils, and arrange some running down the spine of the beast if you like. Finally, chop the jelly (page 10) and spoon it around the edges of the cake for slimy water.

Zebra Desserts

Pictured on page 53

Makes 8

> 250 g (8 oz) can of pineapple rings
> 1 Chivers pineapple jelly
> 284 g (10 oz) can of Hartley's blackcurrants
> 1 Chivers blackcurrant jelly
> 250 g (8 oz) can of fruit cocktail
> 1 Chivers lemon jelly
> 150 ml (¼ pint) double cream, whipped
> 8 sponge finger biscuits, to serve

Drain the pineapple. Make up the juice to 450 ml (¾ pint) with hot water and dissolve the pineapple jelly in it. Leave to cool. Chop up the pineapple and divide it evenly between 8 tall dishes. Add the jelly and then leave the glasses in a cool place for the contents to set.

Repeat the process with the blackcurrants and blackcurrant jelly, again leaving the dishes aside for the jelly to set. Repeat with the fruit cocktail and lemon jelly. Decorate the desserts with whipped cream and serve each with a sponge finger biscuit.

The Desert Island Birthday Cake

Basic recipes: Sponge Cake Mixture (page 8)
Buttercream Mixture (page 9)

---

butter, for greasing
1 quantity Sponge Cake Mixture
50 g (2 oz) digestive biscuits
75 g (3 oz) plain chocolate
1 quantity Buttercream Mixture
4 tablespoons Chivers lemon curd
blue food colouring
2 tablespoons soft light brown sugar
small chocolate fish or shell sweets
To complete
small stick and green crêpe paper, for the palm tree
small box covered in foil, for a treasure chest

23 cm (9-inch) square cake tin
25 cm (10-inch) square cake board

Preheat the oven to Gas Mark 4/180°C/350°F, and grease and base-line the cake tin. Put in the sponge mixture, spread it to the sides, then hollow out the centre slightly. Bake for about 45 minutes until golden-brown and springy to the touch. Turn out on to a wire tray to cool.

Grease a sheet of greaseproof paper and put it on a tray. Roughly break up the biscuits and pile them on to the paper. Melt the chocolate in a bowl suspended over a pan of hot water; then pour the chocolate over the biscuit pile, so that the pieces are almost covered, and stick together to resemble a rocky island. Leave to set.

Split the cake, which is to be the sea, horizontally, spread it with a little of the buttercream and the lemon curd, sandwich the pieces back together, and put the cake on the cake board. Roughly mix blue colouring into the remaining buttercream, and spread it over the cake for the sea, leaving a space clear on one side for the island.

When the chocolate has set, peel the paper off the biscuit mound and position the island on top of the cake. Surround it with light soft

The Desert Island Birthday Cake

brown sugar, for sand. Make a palm tree from the stick and crêpe paper and place it on the island, with a small treasure chest, if possible. Finally, scatter the chocolate fish or shells on the shore. You could also make a few black card shark fins for the sea!

Tropical Cream

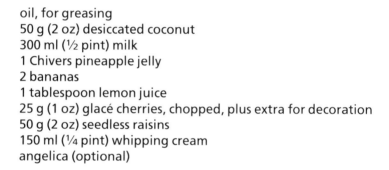

Pictured on page 49

Serves 6

oil, for greasing
50 g (2 oz) desiccated coconut
300 ml (½ pint) milk
1 Chivers pineapple jelly
2 bananas
1 tablespoon lemon juice
25 g (1 oz) glacé cherries, chopped, plus extra for decoration
50 g (2 oz) seedless raisins
150 ml (¼ pint) whipping cream
angelica (optional)

1.2 litre (2-pint) jelly-mould

Lightly oil the jelly-mould. Put the coconut and milk into a pan, bring the liquid to the boil and then leave it on one side for at least 10 minutes, to allow the coconut flavour to infuse into the milk.

Dissolve the jelly in 150 ml (¼ pint) hot water and leave until the jelly cools and starts to thicken. Meanwhile, slice the bananas and mix them in the lemon juice, with the glacé cherries and raisins.

When the jelly is ready, carefully stir in the coconut milk, with the bananas, cherries and raisins. Whip the cream until it just holds its shape and, with a metal spoon, fold it into the other ingredients. Pour the mixture into the mould and leave it in a cool place overnight to set.

Next day, turn the mould out on to a plate and decorate with glacé cherries and angelica, if you like.

The Mad Hatter's Hat Birthday Cake

Pictured on page 56/7

oil, for greasing
2 Chivers pineapple jellies
385 g (15 oz) can of pineapple rings in syrup
glacé cherries
angelica
8 trifle sponges
To complete
a long piece of pretty ribbon
a fresh flower

21 cm (8½-inch) sandwich tin
1 litre (1¾-pint) pudding basin

Lightly oil the tin and basin. Make up the jellies, using the juice from the pineapple rings, and divide 150 ml (¼ pint) between the two containers, so that the bottom of each is thinly covered. Leave to set. Cut three pineapple rings into thirds and, when the jelly in the tin is set, arrange the rings around the outer edge, with glacé cherries and angelica in between. Pour over another layer of jelly and again leave to set.

Place a complete ring of pineapple in the bottom of the basin and use the rest of the pineapple, with more glacé cherries and angelica, to decorate the walls of the basin. Pour in enough jelly to hold the fruit in position and leave to set. Crumble the trifle sponges and mix them into the remaining jelly. When the jelly is set in both the tin and basin, divide the remaining jelly between them. Leave both jellies to set overnight.

Next day, turn the jelly in the tin out on to a serving plate. Carefully turn the basin jelly on to the centre to form the crown of the hat. The easiest way to do this is to turn the basin jelly on to a small dampened plate and then, from the plate, slide it into position. Encircle the hat with the ribbon and lay the fresh flower on the brim.

The Fort Birthday Cake

Basic recipes: Sponge Cake Mixture with chocolate flavouring (page 8)
Buttercream Mixture (page 9)

---

butter, for greasing
1 quantity Sponge Cake Mixture with chocolate flavouring
40 g (1½ oz) cocoa powder
1 quantity Buttercream Mixture
2 packets chocolate finger biscuits
small slab of plain chocolate, for the door
25 g (1 oz) desiccated coconut
brown and green food colouring
soft light brown sugar, for sand (optional)

20 cm (8-inch) square cake tin
28 cm (11-inch) square cake board

Grease and base-line the tin. Preheat the oven to Gas Mark 4/180°C/350°F. Turn the cake mixture into the tin, spread it to the sides then hollow out the centre slightly. Bake for 45–50 minutes. Turn the cake out on to a wire tray to cool.

Leaving a 3–4 cm (1–1½ inch) border, cut the centre from the cake. Cut this piece into 9 squares. Beat the cocoa powder into the buttercream and then spread a little on the board. Carefully lift the cake 'frame' on to the centre. Spread the top with buttercream, then position the cake squares, one on each corner and one in the centre of each wall, to give 8 turrets. Spread the cake with buttercream.

Along three walls position the chocolate finger biscuits, with whole biscuits covering the turrets and halved biscuits covering the lower walls. Cover the fourth side in the same way, but leave the centre turret. Stick the slab of chocolate to this to form the door, with a finger biscuit across the top for the cross beam. Colour the coconut brown and green to look like grass (page 10) and scatter it around the fort. Soft light brown sugar can be used for sand. Finally, position cowboy and Indian models to show that the fort is under attack.

Sausages (on Sticks) (page 55)   Indian Wigwams (page 55)   The Fort Birthday Cake

Parties for 9 & 10-year-olds

By the time children have reached nine or ten years old, very few are interested in the conventional type of party held at home. They seek different ways of celebrating their birthdays, and in this chapter I am going to explore some of the out-and-about treats that are available. Most children of this age still prefer to mix with their own sex, and, if it is a small treat you are organising, I suggest you invite no more than six guests. The length of the celebration rather depends on what form it takes, but normally three hours is quite long enough. Although it is difficult to give the ideal finishing time, as again it depends on the treat, I suggest you make it no later than 8 p.m. Some parents would be concerned if their children were out later.

The type of invitation you send out depends on the kind of party treat being organised. However, it should clearly state the plans for the day, with the location and approximate timings. Also, it should contain requests for suitable clothing, if appropriate, and finally say whether the child has to be picked up or is being taken home after the celebrations.

IDEAS FOR PARTY TREATS
I have divided the treats popular with this age group into three main groups, each with lots of ideas to choose from. No doubt your child will want to join in the organisation of the treat and this is to be encouraged, as children are much more in touch with the likes and dislikes of their friends.

As to the choice of food to be served, this rather depends on the kind of treat being arranged, its location and the time of year. So I have suggested various types of meals and will leave you to select the one you feel appropriate for your particular celebration. You may decide to take a picnic, have a barbecue at home after the treat, or ask all the guests to a meal before setting off.

When deciding upon the numbers to invite, do bear in mind the cost, as it is not usual to ask for a contribution from other parents. For sporting treats, such as a Football Party, obviously you must have enough guests to make up two teams; if, on the other hand, you are planning a trip to the theatre, the number invited can depend upon the price of the seats, including those for the adults accompanying the children. The other governing factor, when deciding upon numbers for treats away from home, is transport. However short a distance, the children should travel safely. If there is a problem fitting everyone into the cars available, perhaps other parents can be asked to assist.

SPORTING TRIPS

Swimming
Contact your local pool to see what facilities they offer. Some pools are prepared to hire out the entire place for an hour, with inflatables in the water for the children's use, plus the services of the attendant. If this is the case, you could invite about ten children. If you are just taking some friends to the local pool, and the pool is open to the general public, for safety reasons, invite no more than four children.

Horse-riding
This is very popular, especially with the girls. Discuss with the riding stable the ability of the children, and do ensure that they all come in suitable clothes, and that spare riding hats are available, if required.

Pitch and put
Probably the optimum number of children for this treat is six or eight. This means that there are not too many waiting about while others are still playing. As the children finish, enrol their help in sorting out who is the current points leader, and then have a prize for the overall winner, plus a prize for any child who gets a 'hole in one'. Do prepare a wet-weather contingency plan for this treat: ten-pin bowling could be a popular substitute.

Skating
Take the children either ice- or roller-skating, depending on your local facilities. Contact the rink to discuss arrangements. I suggest that you allow about an hour at the skating rink, as some children who are not very experienced may find it quite tiring.

Football, hockey, netball or rounders
These team sports are all popular with boys and girls. They can be

arranged either outside on the local pitch or, if you don't want to risk bad weather, in a local sports complex. Some have halls available for hire where five-a-side games would be ideal. Do have a competent referee and organise the teams before you arrive at the venue, to avoid any argument.

Trampolining

Local sports complexes often permit one of their trampoline rooms to be hired for an hour for a party. Contact the booking officer for details, and don't forget to ask about supervision of the children during the activity.

Bowling

This can be a really good treat that everyone enjoys. Ask enough children to make up two teams, and have a prize for the winners.

ACTIVITY TRIPS

Army party

This party is really more suitable for boys. Suggest that the guests come in camouflage clothes – khaki T-shirt and trousers would be ideal – and then plan a cross-country trek. Make the route as much fun as possible, with small obstacles on the way for the children to overcome. Do check the route as near to the party as possible, in case something has changed, and arrange for a refreshment stop half-way round, with a drink and a bar of chocolate. Serve tea at the end of the trek, with a tank birthday cake as the centrepiece (page 76).

It's a knock out

Not for the faint-hearted, this party needs a tremendous amount of pre-planning and then hard work on the day. However, it can be very successful and such good fun. You must have the use of a large garden, and it can be a good idea to join up with another family, as the more adult help you have the better. Arrange the children in teams of about six and try to plan the games so that at least two members of each team participate each time. Announce the running total regularly and have it displayed clearly for all to see. Suggest that the children wear old clothes, and, if you are going to organise some games involving water, ask them to come with swimming gear and a towel. A barbecue at the end of the activities would bring the whole event to a perfect conclusion, but have plenty of cold drinks available throughout the contest, as the children are sure to get very thirsty.

TRIPS OUT AND ABOUT

Indoors
The choice for indoor visits is enormous. Either select a trip to the theatre or cinema, or take a few children to visit a place of interest, such as a museum. Details of suitable places can be found either in the Yellow Pages, the library or the local paper. Limit the numbers to a maximum of six and, if you choose the theatre, book up well in advance to make sure you get the matinée performance. Take along a small bag of sweets for each child and arrange the birthday tea for either before or after the trip.

Outdoors
Days out to the zoo, a visit to a local adventure playground, a trip down the river or on a steam train all prove very popular. Visit your local Tourist Information Office to find out about all the possibilities in your particular area. These treats are sometimes best limited to small numbers, say two or three children. Many can take the entire day, so prepare a picnic lunch and, in case of inclement weather, be prepared with an indoor contingency plan.

MENU IDEAS FOR 9 & 10-YEAR-OLDS

MENU HOT LUNCH

Choose one of the suggested main courses then
a selection of desserts.

Shepherd's pie, served with peas and carrots

Spaghetti Bolognese, served with salad

Lasagne, served with salad

Royal Raspberry Flan (page 74)

Sparkling fruit ring Set colourful fruit in a Chivers jelly

MENU BARBECUE PARTY

Kebabs Thread a selection of cocktail sausages, pieces
    of green pepper, small onions, bacon rolls and
    mushrooms on to sticks; allow two kebabs per person
    (the Barbecue is pictured on page 72/3)

Sausage twirls Wind rashers of bacon around thin
    sausages, secure with cocktail sticks and barbecue

Barbecue sauce Mix together a jar of Hartley's red
    plum jam, 6 tablespoons of tomato ketchup,
    3 dessertspoons of Worcestershire sauce and
    seasoning; brush over the food on the barbecue

Fried onions

Orange and Strawberry Dip (page 79)

Apple and Mincemeat Slice (page 72)

MENU COLD LUNCH

Sausage ring Make a long sausage roll into a ring-shape, cut slits in its outer edge, then bake as for sausage rolls

Savoury flans Serve up a selection

Pasta salad

Tomato and cucumber salad

Pineapple Passion (page 74)

Blackcurrant pavlova cake Spread a pavlova cake with whipped double cream and top with Chivers blackcurrant Fruit for-all

MENU PICNIC PARTY

Stuffed french bread Scoop out a french loaf, fill with sliced ham, tomatoes, lettuce and potato salad, wrap in foil, and then cut into slices when ready – allow two pieces per person

Scotch eggs Allow one per person

Raw vegetables Pack up a container full of salad vegetables

Flapjacks

Bakewell Tartlets (page 75)

Jelly Pots (page 78)

Crisps

Orange or lemon squash (page 7 for quantities)

RECIPES

Apple and Mincemeat Slice

Serves 8

375 g (13 oz) packet of puff pastry
250 g (8 oz) Hartley's mincemeat
375 g (12 oz) cooking apples, peeled and sliced
a little caster sugar

Preheat the oven to Gas Mark 7/220°C/425°F. Roll the pastry into a rectangle 30 × 35 cm (12 × 14 inches). Cut it in half to make two strips, each 17 cm (7 inches) wide, and place one on a baking tray. Spread this piece of pastry with the mincemeat, leaving a 2 cm (1-inch) border. Arrange the apple slices on top and sprinkle with a little sugar.

Fold the remaining piece of pastry in half lengthways and cut it across the fold at 1 cm (½-inch) intervals, leaving a 2 cm (1-inch) border. Open the pastry out again, and then very carefully lift it over the filling, sealing the pastry edges well with water. Brush the surface with water, sprinkle with sugar and then bake for about 20 minutes or until golden-brown and well risen. Serve cut into slices.

Apple and Mincemeat Slice

Barbecue Sauce (page 71)

Sausage Twirls (page 71)

...abs (page 71)

Orange and Strawberry Dip (page 79)

Royal Raspberry Flan

Serves 8

    1 Chivers raspberry jelly
    150 ml (¼ pint) double cream
    150 ml (¼ pint) soured cream
    25 g (1 oz) caster sugar
    1 large sponge flan (about 25 cm/10 inches in diameter)
    375 g (12 oz) fresh raspberries or 385 g (12 oz) can of Hartley's
       raspberries in syrup, drained

Dissolve the jelly in 150 ml (¼ pint) hot water, add another 150 ml (¼ pint) cold water, and leave the jelly until cold. Whisk the double cream and, when it begins to hold its shape, fold in the soured cream and sugar. Add two-thirds of the jelly, and then leave the filling until it starts to set. Turn this mixture into the flan case and leave in a cool place to set completely. Finally, cover the filling with the raspberries, and glaze with the remaining jelly, which should also be on the verge of setting. Leave overnight. Serve with single cream, if you like.

Pineapple Passion

Serves about 6

    226 g (8 oz) can of crushed pineapple
    1 Chivers pineapple jelly
    1 family-size block of vanilla ice cream
    To decorate
    glacé cherries and angelica

Drain the pineapple, make the liquid up to 300 ml (½ pint) with water and melt the jelly in it. Leave to cool. Divide the pineapple between individual dishes. Cut the ice cream into pieces and whisk it into the jelly. Divide the mixture between the dishes and then leave in a cool place to set. Decorate with glacé cherries and angelica before serving.

Bakewell Tartlets

Makes 12

For the pastry
125 g (4 oz) plain flour
25 g (1 oz) lard
25 g (1 oz) margarine
a little cold water
For the filling
50 g (2 oz) margarine
50 g (2 oz) caster sugar
1 egg
50 g (2 oz) self-raising flour, sifted
25 g (1 oz) ground almonds
1 dessertspoon milk
4 tablespoons Hartley's raspberry jam
For the icing
125 g (4 oz) icing sugar, sifted
50 g (2 oz) flaked almonds, toasted

a fluted pastry cutter
12 small patty tins

Preheat the oven to Gas Mark 5/190°C/375°F. To make the pastry, sift the flour into a bowl. Add the fats, cut into small pieces, and rub them in until evenly distributed. Stir in sufficient water to make a fairly stiff dough. Roll out the dough thinly and cut out fluted pastry rounds a little larger than the patty tins. Re-roll the pastry to cut out the exact number required. Line the tins with the rounds, and then leave the tray in a cool place while making the filling.

Cream the margarine and sugar together until light and fluffy. Beat in the egg, and then stir in the sifted flour, ground almonds and milk. Put a teaspoonful of jam into each pastry case and cover with a heaped teaspoonful of sponge mixture.

Bake the tarts for about 25 minutes until well risen and golden-brown. Leave to cool. Mix the icing sugar with enough cold water to make a fairly soft icing. Ice each tart and sprinkle with toasted almonds.

The Tank Birthday Cake

Basic recipes: Sponge Cake Mixture with chocolate flavouring (page 8)
Buttercream Mixture (page 9)

---

butter, for greasing
1 quantity Sponge Cake Mixture with chocolate flavouring
40 g (1½ oz) cocoa powder
1 quantity Buttercream Mixture
3 tablespoons Hartley's apricot jam
6 digestive biscuits
1 round chocolate-coated biscuit
1 chocolate finger biscuit
liquorice straps or comfits
To complete
toy soldiers

23 cm (9-inch) round cake tin
200 g (7 oz) empty round can
30 cm (12-inch) square or round cake board
a number 8 star nozzle and piping bag

Preheat the oven to Gas Mark 4/180°C/350°F. Grease the tin and can, and line the base of each with a piece of greaseproof paper cut to fit. Grease the paper lining.

Put 1 tablespoon of the sponge mixture into the small can and ease it to the sides; then turn the rest of the mixture into the large cake tin. Spread it to the sides, leaving the centre slightly hollow. Bake the cakes; the small cake will take about 20 minutes, the large cake about 1 hour. Turn them out on to a wire tray to cool.

Beat the cocoa powder into the buttercream, and then spread a thin layer over the cake board. Cut the large cake through, spread it with jam, and then sandwich it back together again. Divide the cake into 3 even pieces, trim off a 1 cm (½-inch) strip along the two side pieces and set aside. Slice a wedge off one end of the centre strip of cake to form the front of the tank. Place the main piece of cake towards the back of the board, and spread with buttercream. Fit the two side

The Tank Birthday Cake

pieces on each side, with their cut surfaces down, to form the track parts of the tank. Cut the wedge-shaped piece of cake into pieces and use it to raise one side of the tank, to give the effect of it travelling over rough terrain. Fit the two strips of trimmings on the top of the tank, and then cover the entire cake with more buttercream. Trim the small cake level, and fit it on top for the turret. Cover this also with buttercream, and position the round chocolate biscuit as the turret lid.

Put the liquorice straps or comfits around the two outer pieces of cake, to represent caterpillar-tracks. Then darken the remaining buttercream with extra cocoa powder. Put the buttercream into the piping bag and, on the sides of the tank track, pipe in the wheels – 5 at the bottom, and 4 on top. Push the chocolate finger biscuit in position on the turret for the gun. Crush the digestive biscuits and scatter them around the board to give the effect of sand, and place some fighting soldiers around the tank.

Jelly Pots

Makes 10

2 trifle sponges
2 trifle sponges
750 g (1 lb 14 oz) can of fruit cocktail

10 × 150 ml (¼-pint) empty yogurt or cream cartons

Cut the sponges into small pieces and divide them between the cartons. Drain the can of fruit cocktail and make the juice up to 300 ml (½ pint) with water if necessary. Melt the jellies in the liquid. Add enough cold water to make the liquid jellies up to 1 litre (1¾ pints) and leave on one side to cool.

Finally, divide the fruit cocktail between the cartons and fill up each carton with jelly. Leave the pots to set in a cool place overnight. To take on the picnic, place the pots in a tin and keep the tin upright. Don't forget to pack teaspoons!

Orange and Strawberry Dip

Pictured on page 72/3

Serves 10

1 Chivers orange jelly
1 large can of evaporated milk, chilled
500 g (1 lb) ripe strawberries or 2 × 284 g (10 oz) cans of
    Chivers strawberries in juice
sponge fingers

Dissolve the jelly in 150 ml (¼ pint) hot water, and then add sufficient cold water to make the liquid up to 300 ml (½ pint). Leave the jelly in a cool place until it is starting to set.

In a large bowl, whip the evaporated milk until it is thick and creamy and has doubled in bulk. Keep 8 strawberries aside for decoration, prepare the rest, and then mash them to a pulp. Stir the jelly and the strawberries lightly and quickly into the whipped milk and turn the pudding into a serving bowl. Leave it in a cool place overnight to set. Decorate with the reserved strawberries, and serve with sponge fingers.

Special occasions

CHRISTMAS AND NEW YEAR — 25 DECEMBER – JANUARY 1

Christmas is a wonderful and exciting time when you can hold lots of different parties. Great fun for children is a Mince Pie and Orange Squash Party, which is really a short get-together – say one and a half hours. Allow about three mince pies and two cups of orange squash per person (page 7). Organise a few games, but also put out your own children's toys and puzzles, so that the children can amuse themselves.

Christmas is also the time for family gatherings, which, with a mix of both adults and children, have to be arranged differently from the traditional children's parties. The classic family party game must be Charades, although games with pencil and paper, such as Consequences, are very popular. The food very much depends on the type and time of the party, so select savoury dishes from other celebration Menus, and serve a selection of desserts. Here are a few suggestions:

MENU CHRISTMAS & NEW YEAR

Savouries Select from other Menus

Christmas Trifle (page 90)

Special Mince Pies (page 91)

Raspberry Crunch (page 87)

Christmas Trifle (page 90)   Special Mince Pies (page 91)   Raspberry Crunch (page 87)

HALLOWE'EN – 31 OCTOBER

This party is more suitable for children over the age of seven as, by this age, they are not too afraid of the dark. Ask everyone to dress in a spooky costume – even the adults should appear as witches or wizards – and begin the party just as it is getting dark. Decorate the room with black cut-out shapes of cats, bats, witches' hats and broomsticks, and try and create an eerie atmosphere in the room with dim lighting. Hollowed-out pumpkins, made into faces, are the traditional lanterns, but, if pumpkins are not available, use large swedes or even jam jars covered in black paper with cut-out shapes. Night-lights are the safest candles to use in these holders, but even so, it is probably safer to extinguish them when party games commence.

Apple Bobbing is the traditional game to play at Hallowe'en. Make sure that the bucket is on a large polythene sheet, in case of splashes. Another popular game is Witches in the Castle (page 92). A treasure hunt in the garden – weather permitting – using only torches, is great fun. Here are a few suggestions for the tea:

MENU HALLOWE'EN

Tasty spiders Fry or bake balls of sausagemeat and, when cold, add eight potato-stick legs and two tomato-ketchup blob eyes, if you wish (pictured on page 85)

Cheese straw snakes (page 30)

Ghost sandwiches Using white bread, make a selection of sandwiches; cut out two ghost shapes from each round and, with food colouring, mark two eyes on each ghost (pictured on page 85)

Spiders' Webs (page 86)

Witches' Ring (page 86)

The Bat Birthday Cake (page 84)

Witches' brew Use food colouring to make lemonade a weird colour (pictured on page 85)

GUY FAWKES – 5 NOVEMBER

Young children are often frightened of fireworks so, for them, it is best to plan the party with a good view from inside. Older children, who will want to be outside, must be aware of the firework safety rules. If you are inviting quite a few children, it is wise to rope off an area around the firework display so that they can be kept well away from any danger, and arrange for two adults only to set off the display.

This is another occasion which is more fun if several families can get together. With the cost of fireworks nowadays, it really is the only way of having a good display. If the families agree, pool all the money to be spent on fireworks and then go and buy them all together. A few really good displays are much more appealing to the children than lots and lots of little ones. Youngsters seem to lose interest quickly, so plan the display to last no longer than half an hour, and have several packets of sparklers to hand out when there's a pause in the display.

Start the party with the lighting of the bonfire and the burning of the guy, so everyone can stand round the fire and keep warm during the firework display. Once the display has begun, start serving food and drinks; these should be warming and easily eaten outside. Make sure the food area is well-lit and away from the display, and provide several litter bins. If you want to give every child a small present, an inexpensive torch will be much appreciated. Hand them out as the children arrive, so that they can use them during the party.

MENU GUY FAWKES

Pizzas Small individual pizzas, or easily managed slices

Sausage candles A cooked sausage pushed into a slice of french bread to represent a candle and holder, with a blob of tomato ketchup on top for the flame

Gingerbread men

Parkin

Apple Mousse (page 88)

Fudge Cups (page 88)

RECIPES

The Bat Birthday Cake

Basic recipes: Sponge Cake Mixture with chocolate flavouring (page 8)
Buttercream Mixture (page 9)

butter, for greasing
1 quantity Sponge Cake Mixture with chocolate flavouring
40 g (1½ oz) cocoa powder
1 quantity Buttercream Mixture
4 tablespoons Hartley's apricot jam
1 glacé cherry, halved
2 slivers of blanched almonds

a large roasting tin
a number 2 writing nozzle and piping bag
a large board, covered with foil

Preheat the oven to Gas Mark 4/180°C/350°F. Grease the tin and line the base with greaseproof paper. Turn the sponge mixture into the tin and spread it to the sides, leaving the centre slightly hollow. Bake for 50 minutes or until the cake is golden-brown and springy to the touch. Turn out on to a wire tray to cool.

Beat the cocoa powder into the buttercream. Split the cake in half horizontally, spread with the jam then sandwich the two pieces back together again. Draw the shape of a bat on a piece of paper and cut it out to make a template. Fit it onto the cake and cut round it. Carefully lift the bat on to the board. Spread the entire cake with buttercream, and then, from some of the leftover pieces of cake, cut out 2 ears. Build up the centre of the bat shape for the body. Cover these pieces with buttercream and rough it with a fork. Add a little extra cocoa to the remaining buttercream, put it into the piping bag, and highlight the wing folds, then pipe around the top and bottom edge of the cake. Position glacé cherries for eyes and almond slivers for teeth.

Ghost Sandwiches (page 82)   Tasty Spiders (page 82)
Witches' Ring (page 86)   Witches' Brew (page 82)   The Bat Birthday Cake

Witches' Ring

Serves 6

oil, for greasing
312 g (11 oz) can of mandarin oranges
1 Chivers orange jelly
2 level tablespoons custard powder
300 ml (½ pint) milk
1 level tablespoon cocoa powder
granulated sugar, to taste

1.2 litre (2-pint) ring mould

Rub the inside of the mould with a few drops of oil. Drain the mandarins and make up the juice to 300 ml (½ pint) with water. Melt the jelly in the juice, then spoon 3 tablespoons into the ring-mould. Leave to set. Make up the custard with the milk and cocoa powder and add sugar to taste. Leave to cool, stirring occasionally so a skin does not form.

Arrange a ring of mandarin pieces in the base of the mould and spoon 6 more tablespoons of jelly on top. Leave to set. Chop the remaining mandarins and stir them into the custard, with the remaining jelly. When the base has set, carefully pour in the chocolate jelly mixture and leave overnight to set completely. Next day, turn the mould out on to a plate, and decorate with chocolate cats.

Spiders' Webs

Makes 8

1 Chivers lemon jelly
376 g (13 oz) can of crushed pineapple
150 ml (¼ pint) natural yogurt

150 ml (¼ pint) double cream or dessert topping
4 tablespoons redcurrant jelly, sieved
a few small sweets

8 dishes
a small greaseproof-paper piping bag

Dissolve the jelly in enough hot water to make 300 ml (½ pint). Leave to cool, then stir in the pineapple with its juice, and the yogurt. Divide the mixture between 8 dishes and leave to set.

Whip the cream or dessert topping until stiff and spread it over the top of each dessert. Put the redcurrant jelly into the piping bag, snip off the tip, and then pipe a spiral around the top of each. With a skewer, draw 6 lines from the centre outwards on each dessert to give a web effect. Decorate with small sweets, if liked. Keep cool until required.

Raspberry Crunch

Pictured on page 81

Serves 6

1 Chivers raspberry jelly
284 g (10 oz) can of Hartley's raspberries
50 g (2 oz) margarine
2 tablespoons golden syrup
125 g (4 oz) cornflakes
150 ml (¼ pint) raspberry yogurt

Dissolve the jelly in 150 ml (¼ pint) water. Make up to 750 ml (1¼ pints) with the raspberries and their juice and water. Leave in a cool place to set.

Melt the margarine and syrup in a saucepan, and then stir in the cornflakes. When cool, chop the jelly and then layer it into 6 dishes with the yogurt and the cornflake mixture.

Assemble the desserts only about an hour before the party starts, so that the cornflake mixture doesn't soften.

Apple Mousse

Serves 8

2 tablespoons Hartley's apricot jam
500 g (1 lb) apples, cooked and puréed
1 Chivers lemon jelly
grated rind and juice of 1 lemon
2 eggs, separated
150 ml (¼ pint) whipping cream
1 dessert apple
3 glacé cherries

Stir the jam into the apple purée while it is still warm. Dissolve the jelly in 150 ml (¼ pint) hot water, and stir in the lemon rind and most of the juice. Add the jelly to the apple mixture, then beat in the egg yolks. Leave the mixture to cool. When the apple mixture is starting to thicken, whisk the cream until it is thick enough to hold its own shape and whip the egg whites until stiff. Fold them both into the apple and turn the whole mixture into a serving dish. Leave overnight to set. To serve, core and thinly slice the dessert apple, toss the slices in the rest of the lemon juice, then arrange them overlapping around the centre of the dish, with the glacé cherries in the middle. Serve with brandy snaps.

Fudge Cups

Makes 6

1 Chivers orange jelly
50 g (2 oz) plain chocolate
50 g (2 oz) soft light brown sugar
50 g (2 oz) butter
2 eggs, separated
75 g (3 oz) Maryland Cookies, crushed
1 chocolate flake bar, crumbled
crystallised orange slices

Over a low heat, dissolve the jelly in 150 ml (¼ pint) water, add the chocolate and sugar, and when they have melted, stir in the butter. Stir the mixture until it is smooth, and then remove the pan from the heat. Beat the egg yolks together and then gradually beat in the hot liquid. Leave to cool. When the mixture is starting to set, whisk the egg whites until they form soft peaks, then carefully fold them in. Divide the crushed biscuits beween 6 serving dishes, pour the mousse on top and leave in a cool place overnight to set. To decorate, sprinkle the surface of each with some of the flake, and add an orange slice.

Christmas Trifle

Pictured on page 81

Serves 8

1 Chivers strawberry jelly
385 g (13 oz) can of Hartley's strawberries in syrup
1 jam-filled swiss roll, sliced
3 tablespoons custard powder
2 tablespoons caster sugar
600 ml (1 pint) milk
150 ml (¼ pint) double cream
glacé cherries and angelica, to decorate

Make up the jelly. Drain the can of strawberries and reserve the syrup. Arrange the swiss roll slices around the edge of a glass serving bowl. Put the strawberries into the base and pour over 150 ml (¼ pint) jelly; leave to set. Pour the rest of the jelly into a shallow tin and leave overnight.

Next day, put the custard powder and sugar into a saucepan, blend in a little of the milk and, when a smooth paste is formed, stir in the rest of the milk. Put the pan over the heat, and stirring all the time, bring the custard to the boil. Boil for a minute to thicken, and then leave on one side, stirring it occasionally, until cool. Pour over the set jelly.

Whip the cream until stiff, and pipe large swirls around the edge of the bowl. Chop the jelly (page 10) set in the shallow tin and pile it into the centre of the dessert. Decorate with cherries and angelica.

Special Mince Pies

Pictured on page 81

Makes 18–20

300 g (10 oz) plain flour
1 dessertspoon caster sugar, plus extra for sprinkling
a pinch of salt
150 g (5 oz) margarine, plus extra for greasing
75 g (3 oz) lard
grated rind of ½ orange
1 tablespoon orange juice
1 egg, separated
250 g (8 oz) Hartley's mincemeat
brandy butter, to serve

2 fluted pastry cutters
20 patty tins

Preheat the oven to Gas Mark 5/190°C/375°F. Grease the patty tins. Sift the flour, sugar and salt into a bowl. Add the fats, cut into small pieces, and rub them in until they resemble breadcrumbs. Stir in the orange rind, and then bind the ingredients together with the orange juice, egg yolk and most of the egg white, leaving a little for glazing.

Roll out the dough on a lightly floured surface and, using fluted pastry cutters, one a little larger than the tins and one slightly smaller, cut out an equal number of rounds. Gather up the remaining pastry, re-roll it and cut out more rounds. Use the larger rounds to line the tins. Place a spoonful of mincemeat in each and cover with the smaller rounds, sticking the lids into position with water. Seal the edges well, and then brush the tops of the pies with egg white and sprinkle with caster sugar.

Bake for 20 minutes or until golden-brown. Cool on a wire tray, and serve with brandy butter, if liked.

Party games

Here are just a few games that I have found very popular with children.

WITCHES IN THE CASTLE
Age range: 4–8 years
Number of players: unlimited
Equipment: a bunch of keys and a blindfold

The children sit in a circle with one child, the 'witch', in the middle. Blindfold the witch and place a bunch of keys in front of him or her. Point to a child in the circle, who then creeps around the outside of the other children, through the gap in the circle and right up to the witch, to try and grab the keys without being heard. If the witch thinks he or she hears the 'intruder' and correctly points to him or her, the child trying to get the keys has to sit down again, and another intruder is selected. The child who succeeds in grabbing the keys, without the witch pinpointing his or her position, becomes the next witch.

PASS THE PARCEL
Age range: 3–10 years
Number of players: unlimited
Equipment: a small present wrapped in a vast quantity of paper;
    forfeits, i.e. slips of paper with instructions (optional); music; a large
    box or sack for rubbish

This is an ideal game to play after tea to keep the children quiet for a while. Wrap the parcel in many layers of paper and, if the children are old enough, put forfeits in some of the layers. Forfeits could be: hop round the room like a frog; sing a nursery rhyme; pick up six peas with a straw; tell a joke. Get the children to sit in a circle and to pass the parcel from one to the other as long as the music is playing. When the music stops, the child left holding the parcel unwraps one layer, and performs the forfeit, if there is one. The child who takes off the last piece of paper wins the present. Get the children to put the rubbish in the box or sack.

MUSICAL BUMPS
Age range: 3 and over
Number of players: unlimited
Equipment: music

Children start marching around the room when the music starts. When the music stops, they sit on the floor as quickly as possible. In each round, the last child down is out, until only one child is left as the winner.

There are several variations on this theme:

Musical chairs Enough chairs for every child but one are arranged in a row, facing alternately backwards and forwards. When the music starts, the children march round the chairs. When the music stops, each child races for a chair. The child left standing drops out. When the music starts again, a chair is removed, and so on, until only one chair is left. The child who sits on it is the winner.

Musical islands Sheets of newspaper to symbolise islands are arranged on the floor, one fewer than the number of children. The children 'swim' round them while the music is playing. Then, as soon as it stops, each has to find a free sheet. The child left standing drops out. A sheet is removed, and so on, until only one player, the winner, is left.

Musical statues The children dance around the room to music. When the music stops, they have to stand quite still. Anyone who moves is out, and the child remaining at the end is the winner.

JUMBLE SALE
Age range: 4–10 years
Number of players: teams of at least 4
Equipment: lots of old clothes

This game is especially enjoyable if the party is held in a hall, as you need quite a bit of space. Arrange the teams at one end of the hall. At the other, put out a pile of old clothes for each team. At the signal to start, a member of each team runs to the pile, selects an item of clothing, puts it on and then runs back, when the next member of the team takes over. The winning team is the one that finishes dressing first.

HUNT THE PAIRS
Age range: 4–10 years
Number of players: unlimited
Equipment: paper bags and pairs of small objects

This is a good game to play when everyone is arriving. Give each child a paper bag containing about six small objects, such as a matchstick, button, paperclip, safety pin, coin, rubber-band, and so on. Hide identical objects around the house and garden, and send the children off to find exact pairs.

DONKEY'S TAIL
Age range: 4–8 years
Number of players: unlimited
Equipment: a large blackboard and a piece of chalk, or a picture of a donkey without a tail, a cardboard donkey's tail with a piece of blu-tack attached, and a blindfold

If you are using the blackboard, draw a donkey without a tail on it. Each child is blindfolded in turn and given the chalk (or given the cardboard donkey's tail) to put the donkey's tail in what they think is the correct spot. The child who gets closest is the winner.

This game can be adapted to fit in with several of the theme parties described in the book. For example, you could put the bow-tie on the teddy bear (page 14), or put the parrot on the pirate's shoulder (page 31), or on the palm tree (page 50).

FANNING THE FISH
Age range: 3–7 years
Number of players: unlimited
Equipment: tissue-paper fish and old newspapers

Cut out a tissue-paper fish about 20 cm (8 inches) long and 10 cm (5 inches) wide for each child. Give the children a folded newspaper each to use as a fan. Line the players up, and, at the signal to start, encourage them to fan their fish across the room, by waving the newspapers. Anyone caught touching their fish is out. The first child across the room is the winner.

ADVERTISEMENTS
Age range: 8 and over
Number of players: unlimited
Equipment: advertisements; pencils and paper

Cut out a number of popular advertisements from magazines, removing the product names. Number each advertisement, and then stick them up around the party room. As the guests arrive, give each a pencil and paper and set them the challenge of naming as many of the products as possible. The winner is the one with the most correct answers.

KIM'S GAME
Age range: 6–10 years
Number of players: unlimited
Equipment: paper and pencil, a cloth and a tray of at least 12 small
    objects, such as a torch, button, piece of string, matchbox, and so
    on

Give everyone paper and pencil, and sit them in a circle. Bring in the tray, covered with a cloth. When everyone is ready, remove the cloth for 30 seconds. Take the tray away again and the players have to write down as many objects as they can remember. The player who remembers the most is the winner.

DEAD LIONS
Age range: 4–8 years
Number of players: unlimited
Equipment: none

All the children lie on the floor with their eyes closed as 'dead lions'. If any of the lions move, they are out. The last player lying on the floor is the winner.

Index

Design: Ken Vail Graphic Design
Photography: Eric Carter
Food preparation for photography:
   Berit Vinegrad
Styling: Judy Middleton White
Typesetting: Goodfellow & Egan,
   Cambridge
Printed and bound in Great Britain by
   The Eagle Press plc, Blantyre